Thomas Kinsella

GODHEAD

Thomas Kinsella

Peppercanister 21

Peppercanister

Distributed in Ireland by
The Dedalus Press,
24 The Heath, Cypress Downs, Dublin 6W

in the United Kingdom by
Carcanet Press Limited,
4th Floor, Conavon Court,
12-16 Blackfriars St., Manchester M3 5BQ

in the United States & Canada by
Dufour Editions Inc.,
P.O.Box 7, Chester Springs, Pennsylvania 19425

First published 1999

The Dedalus Press
ISBN 1 901233 34 0 (paper)
ISBN 1 901233 35 9 (bound)

Carcanet Press Ltd
ISBN 1 85754 438 2 (paper)
ISBN 1 85754 437 4 (bound)

Printed in Ireland by Colour Books Ltd.

The Dedalus Press receives financial support from
The Arts Council, An Chomhairle Ealaíon, Dublin.

To the memory of Liam de Paor

CONTENTS

High Tide : Amagansett

The ocean swell mounted, approaching the land;
folded in a long crest, whitening along its length;
and dismantled in thunder up the miles of shore,

the spent uproar delivering its remains
into the remains of the last wave returning against it
to the sea, into the throat of an overhanging wave.

The waves, arguing among themselves
along the slope of shore, are alive,
hurrying in disorder between two stillnesses :

at a depth without light, beyond the first stir of unrest;
and in the thin shape of sea water
halted on the sand at my bare foot

discovering the first thought of withdrawal.

San Clemente, California : a gloss

All metre and mystery
touch on the Lord at last.
The tide thunders ashore
in praise of the High King

shaking the night air
along the distant seafront.
A breath
at my open window.

Godhead

Trinity

The Father
in absolute beauty, absolutely still.
He has done everything in His power.

The Son hanging on high,
reconciling the Father's requirements
with His capacity.

The Third Person
holding Its breath.

Father

I found Him at the end of the passageway,
enthroned, with head hanging and stone beard.
And laid my briefcase on His stone knees.

                *

Father, bent above Thyself
still as at the beginning;
reflecting on Thine own image
— not yet perfect. Lost in the work.

Be mindful of us, who were among
the last of Thy thoughts, and who also know
how it is possible to grasp completely
while remaining partly incapable.

And He responded not in the sound of thunder
or in the voices of angels or in similitudes
but bodily, with a palpable tongue
trafficking in carnal things.

                *

I put my hand in my bosom.

When I took it out

behold, it was leprous as snow.

And the Father said : *Put thine hand*

in thy bosom again. And behold

it was turned again as my other flesh.

And I said : O my Father,

Thou hast spoken to Thy servant !

But I am slow of speech — they will not believe me.

And His anger was kindled against me.

And He said :

Who hath made thy mouth?

*

I offered my prayer up

unfinished. And heard

my own voice reply :

Proclaim Our incompleteness, only begotten.

While I prepare

the next part of the Prayer.

*

I set the last piece back in place

to seal Him in.

His stone hand flat on my books.

Son

She was sitting pale at the window
with her palms open upward on her lap;
her face set in consent, with a sealed smile.

He is gone, the blood beating
in the veins thick at His temples;
leaving two memories in her flesh.

A Stranger fallen across her
in fierce relief, without love.
And the Adjustment in her body.

*

The Baby's head was resting
on Its mother's neck, starting to doze off.
Put It down carefully, without waking It up.

It gave a little jaded cry.
Hold It close.
It started to doze off again. Put It down carefully.

There was a whinge of protest.
Leave It, shutting the door quietly.
Sometimes you have to let them cry it out.

It lay there by Itself without a stir.
Then started crying in earnest,
the little Face wrinkled back in hatred.

*

The Head hanging on one side,
signifying abandonment.

The Arms hammered open,
signifying acceptance.

The Smile empty,
signifying passive understanding.

Spirit

A wind that passes and does not return.
Disturbing a few particles
loose on the desert.

Dust of our lastborn.

GODHEAD is number 21 in the Peppercanister series by Thomas Kinsella. It is set in 12 point Times New Roman and published in a paperback edition of 1,200 copies and a bound edition of 350 copies.

First published May 1999

Quotation in "San Clemente, California : a gloss" from: "A Defence of Poetry", Giolla Brighde Mac Con Midhe; 13th century. Translation, Thomas Kinsella.

Cover: from *Mandalas of the Celts*; Klaus Holitzka (Sterling; NY; 1996)